Presenting the Outstanding Women of the Bible

The Bible is the story of God's dealings with his people. This story is like a picture God painted for all the world to see. God wanted to show everyone, everywhere, how much he loves ordinary people, and how he can make wonderful things happen through ordinary lives.

Israel was a nation with laws and traditions which gave men the leadership in government and family life. However, Israel's history is full of stories of women. Some of these women rose to become leaders. Others shaped and changed the life of their nation as they stayed in the background. These stories stress the unique influence women can have on history.

In Israel, the influence of women might have been limited by the customs and laws of their country, or by personal things such as the amount of money they had, the type of education, their husband's position, or the number of children in the family. But in these stories we meet woman after woman who, in spite of outward hindrances, was limited only by the degree of her faith in God or by the degree of her determination to use the gifts he gave her.

We hope this book will make you eager to be used by God, and help you to believe more than ever before that you can be all God made you to be.

DEBORAH
A woman who brought an entire nation back to God
Retold by Marlee Alex
Illustrated by José Pérez Montero
© Copyright 1987 by Scandinavia
Publishing House, Nørregade 32, DK-1165 Copenhagen K.
English-language edition published 1988
through special arrangement with Scandinavia
by WM. B. Eerdmans Publishing Co.,
255 Jefferson Ave. S.E., Grand Rapids, Michigan 49503
All rights reserved
Printed in Hong Kong
ISBN 0-8028-5027-8

Deborah

A woman who brought an entire nation back to God

Retold by Marlee Alex
Illustrated by José Pérez Montero

William B. Eerdmans Publishing Company
Grand Rapids, Michigan

N ot a cloud was in sight as little Deborah peered out of the goatskin tent. The sun poured diamond beams from the sky over the rocky cliff and spilled them onto the sand before her. Heat waves shimmered across the horizon. The girl's small hands fumbled for her head covering and pulled it over her face. Nearly hiding her eyes, the billowy, white fabric protected her from the glare of the light. She flapped the tent door behind her and moved quickly toward the shade of the giant palm tree nearby.

Desert winds blew softly. Grains of sand swirled around Deborah's bare feet as she ran. "Goodbye!" she waved to her father and brothers. They were headed for school in the neighboring village where Deborah's father was a teacher.

Under the wide branches of the palm tree Deborah found refuge from the heat and began to gather the sweet-tasting palm dates lying on the ground around her. The huge, prickly trunk of this tree had often been her backrest on cool evenings. For as long as she could remember, her family had eaten their evening meals here and talked about the boys' days at school.

Deborah wished she could go to school. But she knew that girls in Israel, the country where she lived, had to stay home and help with household chores. In the evenings, Deborah often asked her father many questions. She wondered about the God of her father, whose name was Jehovah. No one dared say this name out loud. Jehovah was a powerful and mysterious God. "But He loves His people, the children of Israel," Deborah's father had told her.

"I want to know this God myself," Deborah often thought.

One evening, Deborah was playing hide-and-seek with her brothers among the neighbors' tents. Hiding behind a loose tent flap, she heard a grown-up say, "King Jabin's army passed close to here yesterday."

Another neighbor answered, "Next time it will be our tents they tear down, our women they carry off!" Deborah shuddered. But she soon forgot about it and scampered away to find a better hiding place.

As Deborah grew older, the iron chariots of King Jabin's army often rumbled within hearing distance of where she lived. The camel caravans of merchants and traders were seen less and less often. For the people of Israel, any kind of travel was dangerous. They risked their lives even when visiting the wells in the countryside. Enemy soldiers hid in the hills with bows and arrows, waiting to attack those who came to draw water.

With each passing year, the village of tents where Deborah lived dwindled. Many of the tent dwellers pulled up stakes and moved to the cities. "We are tired of being afraid," they told those who stayed behind. "The stone walls of the city will keep us safe."

Deborah heard the villagers complaining as they packed their things. "The gods are deaf. They accept neither our sacrifices nor our prayers."

"Still, we may be no safer in the city," they admitted. "King Jabin's army threatens it at his slightest whim. City people are just as afraid as we are."

"That's right, we are never safe, not even in our own country. King Jabin and the heathen Canaanites are pressing in on us from all sides, making life miserable."

Deborah did not understand everything the villagers said. She did not understand why they reacted to the Canaanites in fear rather than by trusting in God. "Why don't they call on the Lord God?" she asked her father. "Why don't they seek Him, the only One who can help?"

Deborah's father was silent for a long, long time. "They have turned from Him," he answered at last. "They have forgotten His name. In the days of peace, they grew tired of Him and discarded Him like an old coat. They chose new, heathen gods. Now that there is trouble, they are ashamed to call on Him again."

"Then, is there no hope for Israel?" asked Deborah.

"There is always hope, Deborah," her father replied. "We must ask God to make us wise and give us a brave leader."

Deborah kept asking questions as she grew up. Her questions were sometimes difficult to answer. Her father taught her from the holy Scriptures and repeated the stories that he had heard from his father.

There came a day when Deborah's father noticed Deborah actually beginning to answer her own questions. She seemed to have wisdom concerning things even he had wondered about. Deborah began talking to the people in the tent village around her, challenging them to trust in the one true God.

"How can she be so confident?" the villagers asked one another. "Where does she get such courage?"

Before long, people in other villages of Israel heard about this young woman named Deborah, who lived near the great palm tree between Ramah and Bethel. They wanted to listen to her. Some of these people had seen loved ones hurt by King Jabin's soldiers. Others were tense and angry, for the Canaanites living in the hill country threatened them constantly.

Deborah offered comfort to those who came to her. From the Scriptures she gave them a reason to hope. Deborah believed in the future and in the chance for a better life. But she warned her people to repent and turn from worshipping false gods. She told them that Jehovah, the God of Israel, wanted all their love and trust.

Before long, people began coming to Deborah with their personal quarrels. They believed she could settle their arguments for them. Deborah was wise and patient. She knew the right questions to ask in order to find out who was right and who was wrong. And she never stopped challenging the Israelites to be brave, to destroy their idols, and to pray for deliverance from Canaanite kings like King Jabin.

King Jabin wanted to destroy the government of the Israelites. He routinely ordered his soldiers to ride through their city gates and frighten the judges holding court there. But Jabin never attacked the village court of Deborah. "She is only a woman," he told his general. "She can't possibly cause any trouble. Don't bother with her." But King Jabin was wrong.

Deborah was to become one of the greatest judges Israel had ever had. The place where she held court became famous, known as the Palm of Deborah.

"Lord God of Israel," Deborah prayed at the start of every day, "You know I shall be busy today. I want to speak Your truth. Give me Your wisdom." God gave Deborah His own messages to pass onto the people.

One day, Deborah sent a message to an Israelite named Barak. Barak lived in Naphtali, a neighboring area of the country. When he arrived at Deborah's palm tree, Deborah told him, "The Lord God of Israel has appointed you to raise an army of ten thousand men. He wants you to lead them in an attack against the armies of King Jabin. You are to assemble your troops on the top of Mount Tabor. The Lord Himself will draw Jabin's army to the Kishon River below, led by mighty General Sisera. They will have nine hundred chariots with them. But you and your foot soldiers will win the battle!"

Barak turned pale. He stared at Deborah in astonishment. Barak was brave, but not that brave. He knew very well he needed God's help in every battle. And he knew Deborah was led and directed by God. He swallowed the lump in his throat, then answered, "If you will go with me, Deborah, I will go. But if you don't march alongside the rest of us, then I'm going to stay home."

"All right," Deborah smiled. "I'll start preparing right away. But I tell you, Barak, you will not be the hero. When the battle is over, the honor of the victory will go to a woman!"

Barak thought, of course, that Deborah meant the honor would be hers. He was more than willing to let her be the heroine. He left Deborah's palm and hiked back to Naphtali, where he began to organize an army. Ten thousand men bravely volunteered. Deborah soon joined the men and led them to the top of Mount Tabor.

Word came to General Sisera, leader of King Jabin's army, that a company of foot soldiers was camped at Mount Tabor, intending to provoke a battle. "Ha, ha, ha," laughed General Sisera. "Those fools! They want a battle, do they? Then we will give it to them. Ha, ha, ha! What a battle we will give to them! Servant, sharpen my sword and get the horses ready. We will tear the very feet off those pitiful footmen who think they are so brave!"

King Jabin's army was feared most of all for its terrible iron chariots. Sharp scythes were fastened to the wheels of each chariot. When the chariots were driven into an army of footmen, the scythes could cut quickly through bone and muscle, destroying any enemy. And General Sisera was determined to make full use of the chariots' power.

General Sisera's soldiers rode to the foot of Mount Tabor, close to the Kishon River. The Kishon was really just a narrow stream that trickled toward the valley. Sisera's men could easily drive the horse chariots through it from one bank to the other. As the enemy assembled below, Deborah spoke to Barak on the peak of Mount Tabor. "Have

courage!" she exclaimed. "This is the day of victory over General Sisera. The Lord goes before you. He has prepared the victory. It is time to defeat the enemy!"

Just before daylight Barak and Deborah led their men down the slopes of the mountain. Closer and closer they came to the heavily armed soldiers of King Jabin. Barak's men knew their only advantage was that God stood on their side. Their weapons could never penetrate the armor of the king's soldiers, nor had they any defense against the plunging chariots. They would not even be able to take the enemy by surprise. But Barak's men were ready to do the right thing. Deborah was praying fervently.

Suddenly, it seemed the stars began to fall from the sky, plummeting down like balls of ice and fire. General Sisera's soldiers were thrown into a panic. Their horses stampeded and ran off in all directions. General Sisera jumped from his chariot and fled into the hills as fast as his feet could carry him. The Kishon River swelled, overflowed its banks, and swallowed up those Canaanite soldiers too slow to get away.

Barak's men chased the soldiers who were running into the hills and caught up with them, too! They fought until the last enemy was dead. Only General Sisera managed to get away.

Escaping through the underbrush, Sisera passed the tent of a woman whose husband was friends with King Jabin. The woman's name was Jael.

Jael shouted to Sisera as he ran by, "Slow down! Come into my tent and hide until the Israelites have passed by. I'll give you a cold drink and a place to rest until they are gone!"

Sisera was hot, sweaty, and exhausted. "Oh, thank you," he panted. "I accept your kindness gladly." Then he hurried into her tent. Jael took her finest serving bowl and gave Sisera a refreshing drink. She showed him a place on the floor where he could hide and covered him with a blanket. Before long, Sisera fell fast asleep. But Sisera did not know that at that very moment he was in far greater danger than he had been on the battlefield.

Jael was a strong woman who earned her livelihood making sturdy goatskin tents. And she did not take kindly to the cruel soldiers of King Jabin. Once Sisera began snoring in peaceful sleep, Jael grabbed an iron tent peg and placed the tip of it in front of his ear. With a mighty swing of her hammer she pounded the peg through his head and into the ground. Sisera died instantly. The fame of Jael spread throughout Israel. She became a heroine that day, and the honor of the final victory was gained by a woman, just as Deborah had prophesied.

When the battle of the day was over Deborah wrote a song of praise to God while the impressions of His mercy were fresh on her mind and heart. Deborah put the story of what had happened that day to music so fathers and mothers could sing it to their children and their children's children for years to come. "The Lord is mighty, His presence is with us!" she sang out. "The young leaders of Israel are full of faith and obedient to Him! Those who love Him will shine like the rising sun!"

King Jabin's army never recovered from the defeat by Barak and the men who marched under Deborah's direction. The Canaanite people and their kings became weaker and weaker. The people of Israel grew confident, brave, and strong.

Deborah continued as a judge in Israel. She taught her people that God's presence is the best advantage over any enemy. "But, like Barak's soldiers, you must be determined to use that advantage and carry out bravely what God calls you to do," she often told them.

Deborah set a great example for the men and women of her country and time. And she brought an entire nation back to God.

"Deborah, a prophetess, the wife of
Lappidoth, was leading Israel at that time."
Judges 4:4 (NIV)

You can find the story of Deborah in the Old Testament
in the book of Judges, chapters 4 and 5.